IT WAS NEVER JUST ABOUT THE NUMBERS

Dr. Lisa Hoover

H2 Publishing · 2025

DISCLAIMER AND/OR LEGAL NOTICES:

Acknowledgments

First and foremost, I give thanks to God.
I realize now that I left Him out of my last dedication — and that's not just an oversight, it's a problem. Because God comes first. Always.

To my husband, Ernest — my rock and my champion.
Your quiet power is beyond anything imaginable. God knew exactly what I would need for such a time as this. (Esther 4:14)

To my children — thank you. And to my mama...
I miss her deeply. Her wisdom, her grace. My mother had a grace that defies even the word. She walked with a presence that taught without saying much. Her spirit continues to guide me.

To my grandchild — and to the grandchildren I may never meet —
Know this: your legacy didn't start with me. It's rooted in generations of service, love, and giving back. And the rock-solid foundation beneath it all has always been education.

To my team — which has always been God and my husband — thank you for never letting me forget who I am and what I'm called to do.

To those who thought this was just about numbers — thank you, too.
You reminded me why this work matters.

And to you, the reader — thank you for holding these pages in your hands.
For being bold enough to look deeper, think differently, and reclaim your story.

Because it was never just about the numbers — it's always been about the story behind them

— Dr. Lisa Hoover

TABLE OF CONTENTS

Report Card

580

520

620

680

700

640

700 750

Credit Is Not a Character Test

Let's start with the number. You know the one. The one that people don't say out loud.

That three-digit score that sits at the center of your financial identity, yet tells almost nothing about who you actually are. That number you might avoid looking at, that you've whispered about to close friends or carried like a scarlet letter.

Credit has been made to feel like a moral report card. As if it reveals your honesty, your intelligence, your worthiness. But let me tell you something upfront: credit is not a character test.

It's a score. A formula. A system.

One that was never built for us to win in the first place.

For some of us, credit became a band-aid — a way to bridge the gap between paychecks, or a way to access things we were told we *"should"* have. For others, it became something to fear, avoid, or feel ashamed about. And for many, it was both.

We weren't taught to understand credit. We were taught to chase it. Told to "build it up" but never taught how it's scored. Told to "protect it" but never taught how it can be leveraged. Told to never mess it up — or else.

Let's be honest: for communities of color, the credit system wasn't just confusing — it was punishing.

"In a recent survey, 56% of Americans could not correctly define a credit utilization ratio — yet it's 30% of their score."- SOURCE: National Foundation for Credit Counseling , 2022

So we coped. We got cars in someone else's name. We maxed out store cards and ignored the bills. Or we tried to stay off the radar entirely, thinking that would keep us safe. But silence doesn't protect you in a system that keeps score.

MY ECHO:

Let me be real. My parents didn't dodge calls—we didn't even have caller ID back then. But we knew what time it was. You didn't pick up the phone at certain hours. Everybody knew the bill collectors were calling. That's what they were called: bill collectors. They weren't shy about it either. It wasn't just about money—it was about presence, about fear, about shame that seeped into the walls of our homes.

So when we *whisper* about our score—when we carry debt like a secret illness, when we feel unworthy because of what shows on a report—know that didn't start with you. That's generational architecture. That's legacy without clarity.

And yet, here's what you must know:

Credit is not a character test

That three-digit number is not your moral compass.

It does not measure your intention, your integrity, or your intelligence.

It measures access. It reflects systems. It maps transactions, not truth.

MY ECHO:

When I got my first credit card in college, I didn't use it for groceries or books. I used it for freedom. I wanted to go to the movies without asking. I wanted the outfit even if I didn't need it. I wanted to go on vacation because I could. I wanted to feel grown. I wanted to buy things without checking the price tag. And let me tell you—there was *power in that plastic*... until the bill came.

We were taught to fear credit, not to understand it. Taught to protect the score, not to question the system. Told to build, but never told how. Told to avoid mistakes, but never shown the blueprint.

What if we disrupted that? What if we saw the score not as judgment, but as data? What if we reclaimed it—not because we want to perform perfection, but because we want to fund freedom?

Credit Is Not a Curse

You're not broken because you're in debt. You're not irresponsible because you fell behind. You're not unworthy because the algorithm says so.

You are someone who has lived, loved, lost, survived. And now? You're someone who gets to choose something new.

Imagine:

- You walk into a bank without bracing.
- You apply for funding without fear.
- You talk about credit without whispering.

That version of you already exists. She's not a fantasy—she's a future memory waiting to be lived

MY ECHO:

Today, I talk about credit in rooms that once would have silenced me. I teach it. I explain it. I disrupt it. Because I know how many of us were told to stay quiet, stay small, stay confused. Not anymore.

Because credit doesn't define you. But understanding it can liberate you.

Not so you can brag. Not so you can fit in. So you can move freely. So you can build without begging. So you can stop playing small in a system that was never designed for you to win.

Let's start there

Let's Get Practical

Action Step: Get Your Real Credit Snapshot

Visit annualcreditreport.com and pull reports from all 3 bureaus.

Use a highlighter or pen to mark:

- Late payments
- Collections
- Anything you don't recognize

Then write this sentence: **"What do I want my credit to help me do in the next 12 months?"**

Your credit is a tool.
It's not a mirror.
And it damn sure isn't your value.

Debt Is Not A Dirty Word

Let's start here: debt didn't just show up on a spreadsheet.

For many of us, debt was inherited—not always in dollars, but in thinking, in fears, in patterns. And it looked different depending on who raised you.

MY ECHO:

In my family, money meant ownership.
You talked about land, property, assets.
My husband's family? Money was about
survival—but always with savings in mind.
Both were right. Both were incomplete.
And both were shaped by something older
than we tend to name.

In Black families across the South, debt was not just a personal problem—it was structural bondage. You see it in sharecropping. You see it in slavery. You see it in how freedom was always dangled—but never delivered

When you were enslaved, your labor was considered free, no matter how much you gave.

When you were a sharecropper, you bought goods on credit, thinking you'd pay it off after harvest. But somehow, the math never mathed. Your labor should've covered it in full—and then some. But the store owned the scale, the landowner kept the books, and you stayed trapped in a cycle you didn't create.

Sound familiar?

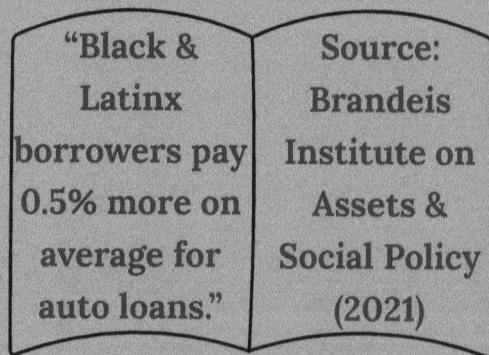

"Black & Latinx borrowers pay 0.5% more on average for auto loans."

Source: Brandeis Institute on Assets & Social Policy (2021)

Today's credit card industry aren't all that different.

This is not a coincidence. It's a continuation.

MY ECHO:

I remember hearing those old stories: going to the store and getting something *"on credit."* That was how folks made ends meet. But nobody explained the long-term cost. Nobody warned that some debts weren't designed to be paid off—they were designed to keep you tethered. That legacy didn't just evaporate. It evolved.

Debt and money got braided together into one unspoken rule: to *owe was to be in trouble.*

And that energy got passed down.

Even when some folks got wise and —said "save a little," "put something away"—the core idea stuck: debt was bad. **Heavy. Dirty. Dangerous.**

But here's the thing no one told us: not all debt is equal. Not all debt is evil. And not all shame is ours to carry.

Debt has a history. And we're not just in it—
we're still climbing out of it.

Let's name it so we can change it.

Debt Is Not a Dirty Word

We've been taught to treat debt like a disease—something contagious, shameful, and to be hidden. But what if debt isn't the problem? What if the story we've been told about debt is what's keeping us stuck?

Debt is not inherently bad. It's a tool. A hammer. It can build. It can destroy. It depends on how you use it—and whether you were ever given a blueprint in the first place.

Most of us weren't.

We learned about debt from watching. From surviving. From piecing together meaning from what wasn't said. We saw debt as struggle. As failure. As something to outrun.

But here's the truth:

Debt is a system. A structure. A reflection of reality— not morality.

We live in a society where the system expects you to have debt.

- You get credit before you get clarity.

- You borrow before you understand the cost.

- You're punished before you even have a chance to learn.

And let's not ignore this: what are the communities most targeted with high-interest, predatory debt? You guessed it- Yes, they are the same ones who were historically locked out of wealth.

It's not a coincidence. It's a design.

So let's be clear:

You are not irresponsible because you have debt. You are not a failure because you're behind. You are not alone if the math "still ain't mathin".

You are someone living in a system that was built to profit from your confusion.

And now you're about to flip that.

Let's Get Practical

✅ List all your debts: credit cards, student loans, medical bills, auto loans, everything.

Next to each, write:

- The total amount owed

- The interest rate

- Whether it was for consumption (to survive) or growth (to invest in your future)

Now, circle one debt that feels like it's draining you the most.

Next, Write this sentence and complete: **"If I could be free from this one debt, it would feel like _____."**

Wealth Isn't Just White or Flashy

Wealth has always worn a costume—especially in our community. It's been packaged, marketed, and sold back to us in pieces—designed for us **not** by us. For many of us, especially in Black and brown communities, we didn't grow up with portfolios—we grew up with presentation. If we couldn't build wealth, we could at least look accomplished. A title here. A zip code there. But this wasn't wealth. It was armor.

MY ECHO:

People have told me for years, "You should lead with it! Put 'Dr.' on everything!" But I've always believed your integrity should speak louder than your intro. Just like money —what you have isn't always who you are.

The title becomes a solo act, utilized like a shield, a door-opener, a declaration that we've arrived. But beneath that, it's also a plea to be safe, respected, seen. That's the tension we're holding—how something meant to protect us also becomes part of the performance

But.

It's not flashy.

It's not loud.

And it definitely isn't white.

Real wealth is quiet. Real wealth holds memory.

MY ECHO:

My grandmother didn't talk about money. She folded it, saved it, stretched it. She kept documents in a lockbox—not because she trusted the system, but because she **didn't**. She made sure Sunday dinner was served and the gas stayed on. That was Wealth. Faithful. Consistent. And invisible to the outside world. Wealth is the pocketful of change my grandfather always had, not for show but to make sure we never went without. If something needed to be taken care of, he could. No fuss. Just provision.

But no one ever called that Wealth. It didn't make magazine covers or get measured in net worth—but it kept generations alive.

And so, we learned to perform too—not for luxury, but for legitimacy. We shaped ourselves to be accepted into rooms that were never built for us. But when *The Cosby Show* aired, it flipped the lens. A Black family— educated, professional, proud, whole. It wasn't fantasy. It was *familiar* to us and foreign to the world. It made people uncomfortable because it disrupted the myth: that wealth had to look a certain way. It mirrored a version of *Black success* that had always been present but rarely seen.

Contrast that with what I remember reading about *Kevin Garnett* —-one of my most favorite players —walking around with stacks of cash. Not because he didn't have access to banking, but because no one had ever taught him to trust the system. Because he knew that the rules of finance weren't built with him in mind. Even in abundance, he had to hold his wealth close. Visibly. Tangibly. Because when you come from a world where nothing is guaranteed, visibility becomes armor.

That's the dichotomy. That's the tension. That's the trap—and for too long, it's been normalized.

Because the truth is: **we inherited Wealth.** Land we once owned. Land we were pushed off. Traditions passed down in kitchens and church pews. Resourcefulness. Life insurance policies that buried generations.

But we also inherited trauma—stories about not enough, about proving, about pretending.

And that's why this chapter matters. Because if we don't pause and examine what we believe about wealth—we'll keep repeating the lie.

We don't just need access. We need language. We need lineage. We need to remember that **Wealth isn't what they sold us**—it's what we survived with.

Generational Wealth has always existed in our communities- it just didn't always look like what the magazines, television ads said it should. And because it wasn't recognized or celebrated, we undervalued it too.

Quiet Power: Wealth Isn't About Status. It's About Safety.

MY ECHO:
The first time I felt wealthy wasn't when I had money in the bank—it was when I realized I could say "no" and still be okay. That I didn't have to shrink, beg, or overextend. That's when I knew: wealth isn't noise. *It's knowing*.

Wealth isn't about being seen. It's about being secure. It's the boundary you set without guilt. The rest you take without apology. The home you build—emotionally, financially, spiritually. And the confidence to say no—without fear that everything will fall apart.

Let's build the kind of wealth we were never meant to see — but always knew was ours.

Let's Get Practical

Action Step: Define Wealth for Your Life

Write down five things that would make you feel financially powerful.

- Circle the ones you already have — and the ones you want to build

- Choose one wealth-building move to research this week: trust planning, insurance, investment account, or business ownership

Wealth isn't performance.
It's protection.
And you don't need a spotlight to build it

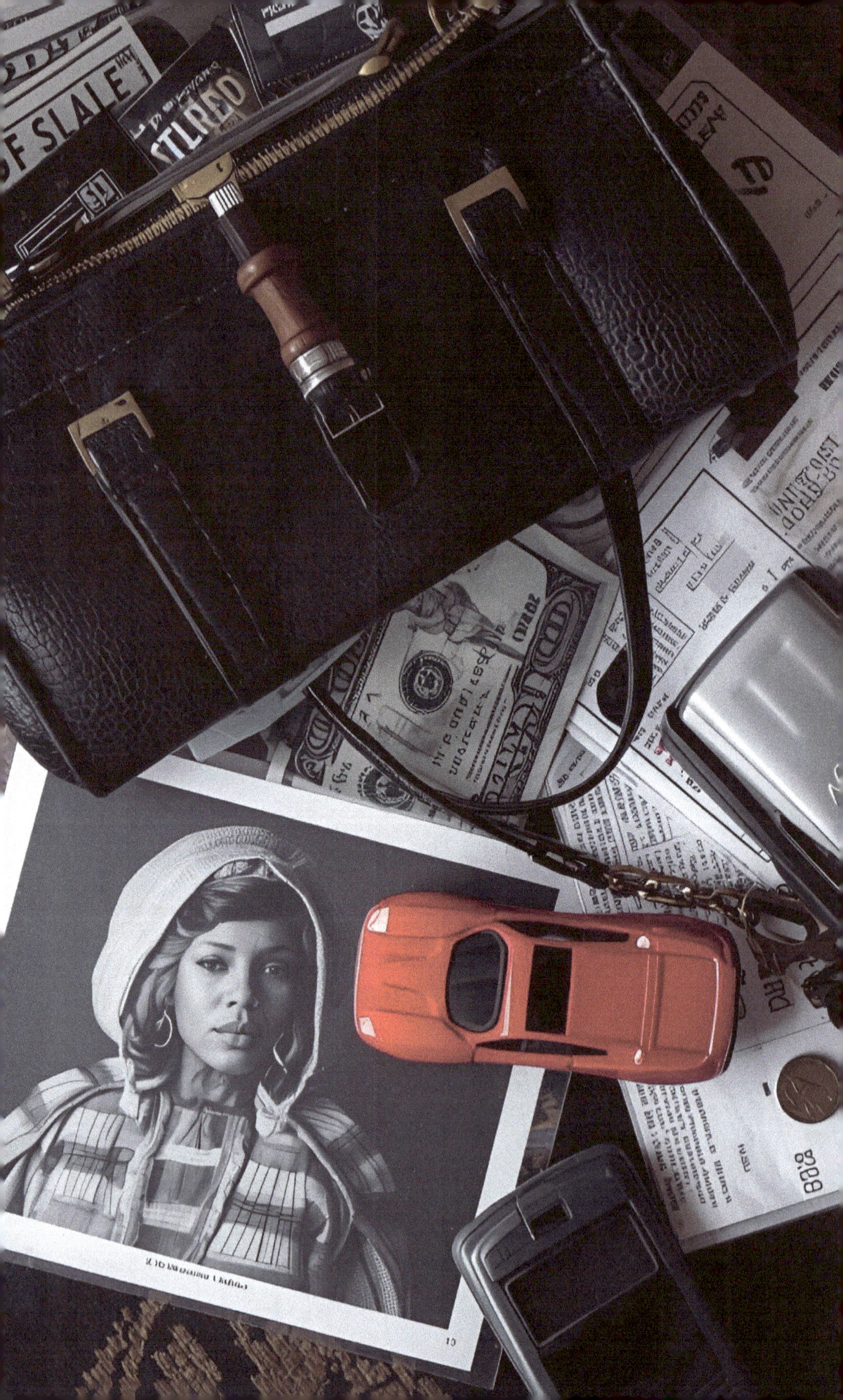
OF SLALE
STLRED

Money Ain't the Whole Story

When my kids were little, I did what every parent does: I bought the toys, the gadgets, the stuff. But at some point, I realized I didn't just want to give them gifts—I wanted to impart something deeper. I wanted to give them what was often shared in our family meetings, but do it differently. I didn't want to lecture—I wanted to talk with them, not at them. I wanted them to understand. I wanted to give them ownership.

So if they liked a movie, I bought stock in the company. If they loved a video game, I bought shares in the platform. If they were into Disney, I didn't just buy the merch—I bought Disney stock. And we talked about it. Why it mattered. What it meant to not just consume, but own.

I never bought them Jordans—not because I couldn't, but because it didn't make sense to me. *Yet,* I was over here buying Gucci bags. So this isn't about throwing shade. It's about evolution. I had to unlearn the idea that value is what you show, and relearn that real value is what you own.

We have to start teaching that early. Make investing a game. Make ownership the flex. Give our kids the language to see money as a seed—not a status symbol.

Money affects everything. *But it isn't everything.*

We forget that money is just numbers—data. It isn't moral. It doesn't care. But somehow, we made it emotional. We turned numbers into identity. Into shame. Into proof. But money is math. And math was never supposed to measure your value.

We weren't taught that. Instead many of us were taught to fear money, to chase it, to silence ourselves around it. We were taught that having money made you "*safe*"—but talking about it made you greedy.

No one ever said money was just energy. Just numbers. Just a tool. Instead, it became a test. A burden. A mirror

The 3 S's: Where Fear Takes Up Residence
Shame. Silence. Scarcity.

Fear doesn't always announce itself.
It doesn't storm into the room screaming.
Sometimes, it sits in the corner and calls itself something else.

We think fear is big and bold—panic, anxiety, a full meltdown.
But fear can also be the reason we laugh off financial conversations,
the reason we delay logging into our bank app,
the reason we accept "I'm bad with money" as identity, not conditioning.

Fear lives in the **quiet.**
In our community, it shows up through three messengers:

✗ Shame – The belief that your struggle is a flaw.
✗ Silence – The absence of language that keeps confusion alive.
✗ Scarcity – The lie that there's not enough, and you're not enough to get more.

These three? ***They're cousins. They travel together.***
And when they move in, they decorate your choices without ever paying rent.

MY ECHO:

I had a conversation—okay, an argument—while previewing this book.

Someone asked me, "Why don't you go deeper on fear?"

And at first, I dismissed it. We'd already said so much.

But later that night, I sat with it.

And I realized something: **I've spent years talking around fear. Not through it.**

We rarely name it for what it is because we've been taught fear means weakness.

But sometimes fear looks like delay. Or performance. Or over-functioning.

And that's when I knew: we couldn't talk about money without talking about this.

Because if we don't name the fear, we never get to reclaim the power underneath it.

We called it *Nothing But Numbers* because that's what money had become—digits on a screen, credit scores on a report, pay stubs in a folder.

But behind every number was a story. A system. A lie.

A *zip code* that determined your mortgage rate.
A *debt* load that whispered shame.
A *salary gap* that was never just about skill.

The numbers were never neutral—they were curated to convince us we were behind.

"1 in 4 Black adults avoids financial services because of past discrimination."
Source: Urban Institute (2021)

And in our communities? Money always felt like Monopoly money. Passed around without weight. Something to play with—but not something we were taught to master.

Change happens... not until we learned to treat it like strategy. Like ownership. Like liberation.

Too often, we treat money like the main character. The destination. The proof. But truthfully? It's just the soundtrack underneath your story. Sometimes loud, sometimes soft—but always in the background, shaping how the scene unfolds.

MY ECHO:

I used to think money would make things make sense. That if I just had enough, I'd feel secure—seen, steady, set. But peace doesn't come from earning. It comes from unlearning.

Because you are more than what you earn.
You are what you build, what you pour into others, and what you refuse to let money steal from you.

We've been sold a dangerous idea: that if you have enough money, you'll be secure, respected, successful. And if you don't? You're failing.

But I've seen people with money and no peace. I've seen people with wealth and no wellness. And I've seen people with limited income who live with deep joy, deep love, and deep impact.

So let this chapter remind you: your financial story matters—but it is not your whole story.

Let's Get Practical

Action Step: Reframe What Success Means to You

- Write down five non-financial things that make you feel secure or free.

- Name one way money could support those things (not replace them).

- Write one sentence: What's one way I can center peace—not just paychecks—this month?

Money matters.
But peace is priceless.

Power Is the Freedom to Move Freely

Power isn't about being in charge of other people. It's about being in charge of yourself.

It's about walking in your truth, choosing how you live, and not needing permission. That's the kind of power I want us to reclaim—not the kind that performs, but the kind that persists. The kind that's quiet, steady, and immovable. Have you noticed? The people who really have power almost never have to prove it.

Credit, debt, and wealth—those are all tools. But power? Power is the thing that decides how we use them. When we move from survival to strategy, we stop letting systems use us and start learning how to move freely within them.

So no, this isn't just about money. It's about Mindset. Memory. Movement. It's about reclaiming the power we've always had but weren't taught to trust.

MY ECHO:

I used to think power meant being the one with the microphone. The one making the rules. But I learned power is quieter than that. It's the ability to say "no" without guilt. To leave the room with your peace intact. To walk away from what doesn't align, not because you're angry—but because you're clear.

Power isn't about dominance. It's not about being the loudest person in the room. It's about Options. Alignment. Autonomy. It's the ability to move without begging, borrowing, or breaking yourself to do it.

When you don't have power, every decision feels like a negotiation. Can I afford this? Will they approve me? Do I have to ask someone else for help? Will this risk ruin me?

But when you do have power? There's room to choose instead of chase.

Power shows up when you can leave a toxic job without panic. When you can walk away from a relationship because you're not financially trapped. When you can break without unraveling.

That's the kind of power we're reclaiming here. Not perfection. Not hustle. Just capacity.

And here's the truth: you don't have to wait to feel like a free person. You just need to remember what's already in your hands.

Walk in Knowledge

🧠 Only 17 states require personal finance classes to graduate high school (Council of Econ Ed 2023)

📉 1 in 5 Black consumers say they were never taught about credit in school — compared to 1 in 10 white consumers. (Urban Institute, 2019)

🏫 Over 70% of Black Americans say they were never taught about credit or investing growing up

Let's Get Practical

Action Step: Identify Where You Want More Power

- Write down three areas where you often feel stuck, small, or silenced.

- Next to each, write what would help you feel powerful in that area.

- Choose one and write: What's one move I can make this month to take my power back here?

Real power isn't about control.
It's about choice.

We were never silent.
We were silenced.

Silence Was Never Safety

We've been told money isn't polite conversation. We've been told not to ask, not to tell, and certainly not to admit what we don't know. But that silence? It costs us.

Here is the thing-Financial shame grows in isolation. And when you mix in cultural pressure, perfectionism, and survival mode—it's no wonder so many of us are carrying quiet financial battles. It's not that we're irresponsible. It's that we've been taught not to talk about it.

💬 **When silence costs us...**

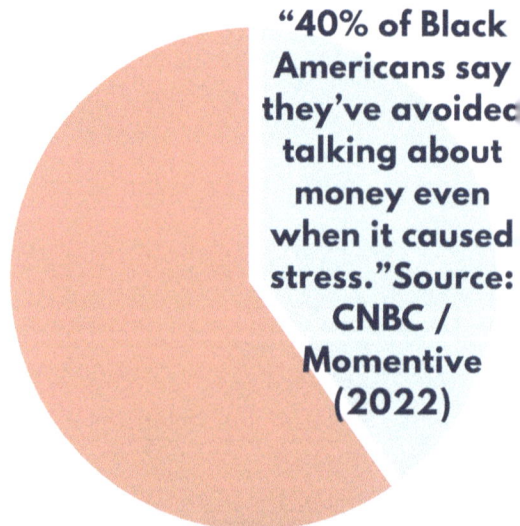

"40% of Black Americans say they've avoided talking about money even when it caused stress."Source: CNBC / Momentive (2022)

MY ECHO:

I grew up around money—but not conversations about it. I could recite "*Money doesn't grow on trees*," but I couldn't explain how a credit score worked. We didn't talk credit. We didn't talk debt. We whispered about bills and prayed about breakthroughs—but never broke the cycle.

Silence became a form of protection, a way to save face. But in the long run, it cost us information, options, and access. Silence kept us from asking for help, from comparing notes, from learning what was normal, what was broken, and what was possible.

.

And the silence didn't just keep us uninformed—it left us fumbling in the dark.
 We were expected to build budgets we were never taught, manage credit we never understood, and make ends meet with tools no one gave us.
 So when the overdraft hit, or the paycheck ran short, or the budget didn't work—it didn't feel like a math problem. It felt like a personal failure

And now? We know better. The cost of silence is too high. It's time we normalized financial transparency— not just in theory, but in practice.

That doesn't mean we spill every detail of our paycheck or our debt-to-income ratio to everyone. But it does mean we stop pretending.

So we *change our language* and ...

We start saying:

- "I don't know, but I want to learn."
- "I made some mistakes, but I'm working on it."
- "I need support, not shame."

Because money doesn't define us. But silence? It isolates us.

And here's the truth: what we don't talk about, we can't change.

Let's Get Practical

Action Step: Start the Money Conversation

- Write down the one money question you were always afraid to ask. (Then Google it. Or better yet, ask someone you trust.)

- Choose a friend, family member, or community space to have one transparent conversation about money this month.

- Bonus: Look for a financial literacy group, class, or podcast you can join to stay in the conversation.

Your silence wasn't your fault.
But your voice? That's your power now

We start here—by talking, by asking, by unlearning.

And then we keep going.

Because the truth isn't in the numbers themselves, but in how we decide to live beyond them.

Conclusion

We were never missing the tools.
We were missing the truth.
You're reclaiming.
You're rebuild.
Not just credit. Not just money. But freedom.

They told us it was about money.
But it was always about control.
They told us it was about debt.
But it was always about denial.
They told us to count.
But not to question what was counted.
They taught us numbers.
But never how they were used against us.
Not Anymore, Not You

Now?
We know better.
And we build different.

Thank you for reading I*t Was Never Just About the Numbers*.

If these pages helped you see your story or your credit in a newD light, please take a moment to share your thoughts in an honestD Amazon review.

Your voice helps others realize they were never the problem — andD that truth belongs to all of us.

As a thank you:
Readers who leave an honest Amazon review can receive aD complimentary **digital version of *The Numbers Don't Lie Journal*** — a guided space to put this work into motion.

How to claim your copy:
Follow the instructions that will be delivered to you by email afterD your review is submitted.

— Dr. Lisa Hoover